The S

Contents

	Page
First satellites	2
First manned flight	4
First moon landing	6
Space shuttle	8
Space telescope	10
Satellites today	11
Robots	12
Planet Mars	13
Space station	14
Space walk	15
Night sky	16

written by Pam Holden

space dog

The Space Age started with the first satellite. It was only as big as a basketball, but the Sputnik satellite flew right around the Earth. The second satellite took a dog for a space ride!

3

The first person to fly into space
was an astronaut from Russia.
He flew around the earth once,
which took one and a half hours.
Then he landed safely back on Earth.

Yuri Gagarin, 1961

Neil Armstrong
Edwin Aldrin

Three United States astronauts were the first people to fly to the moon. They took four days to get there. Two of the men landed on the moon and walked around.

They put up a flag and took some photographs. After two and a half hours, they left the moon. They brought back some moon dust and rocks. There have been five more landings on the moon.

A space shuttle is a spaceship that can fly into space more than once.
It is sent into space by two big rockets.
When it comes back, it lands like a plane.

space shuttle Discovery

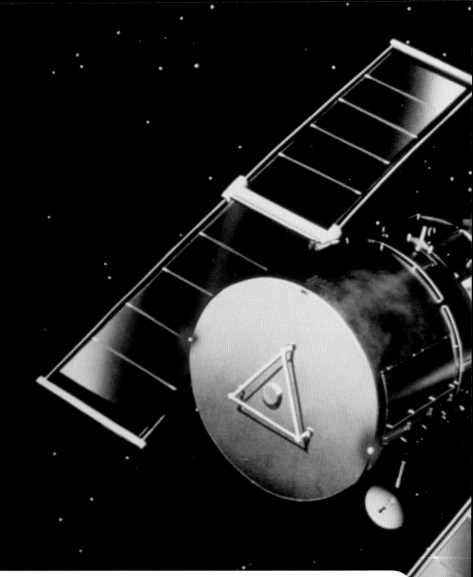

There is a huge telescope, called
Hubble, flying around the Earth.
It takes pictures of the stars and
planets to send back.

Hubble space telescope

There are many satellites flying around Earth. They send back photos and weather reports. Our television and telephone services use satellites every day.

11

Robots are good for exploring space because they don't need to eat or sleep. They aren't frightened of danger, and they can stay in space for a long time.

Mars Pathfinder, 1997

The first landing on a planet was a robot that was sent to Mars in a spacecraft. The robot was like a small car that drove around and took pictures of the planet.

Now there is a space station so that astronauts can find out more about space. They need oxygen tanks to help them breathe. The astronauts float around, because there is nothing to hold things down.

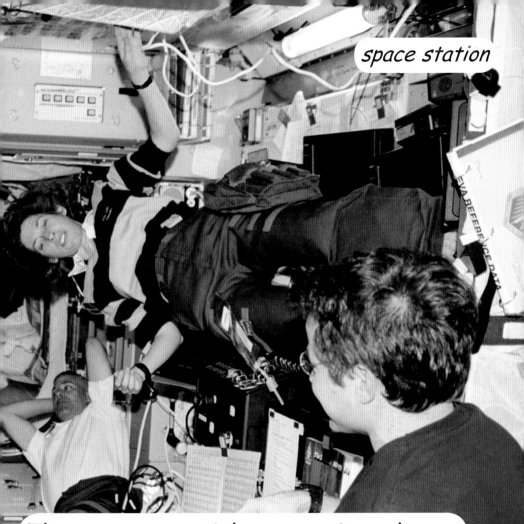

space station

They wear special spacesuits when they walk outside the space station. There is not much noise in space. It can change from very cold to burning hot. Sometimes they live there for many months.

When you look up at night, watch for something moving slowly across the sky. That will be a shuttle, a satellite or a space station flying around the Earth. This is the Space Age!